A *poem by*
Harry Behn

♦

Illustrated by
James Endicott

A Bill Martin Book
Henry Holt and Company • *New York*

TREES

Trees are the kindest things I know,

They do no harm,
they simply grow

And spread a shade
for sleepy cows,

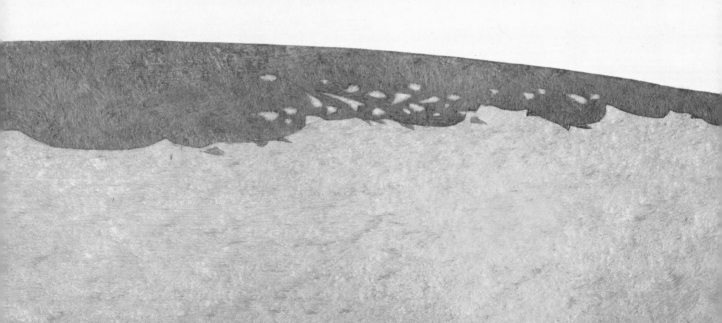

And gather birds among their boughs.

They give us fruit in leaves above,
And wood to make our houses of,

And leaves to burn on Hallowe'en,

And in the Spring
new buds of green.

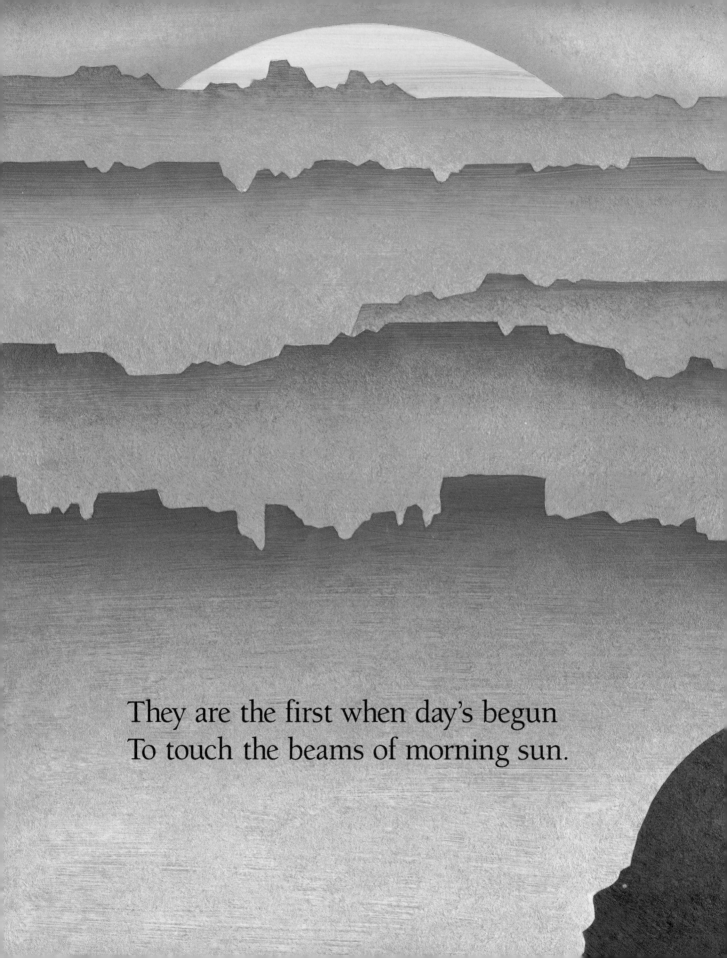

They are the first when day's begun
To touch the beams of morning sun.

They are the last
to hold the light
When evening changes
into night,

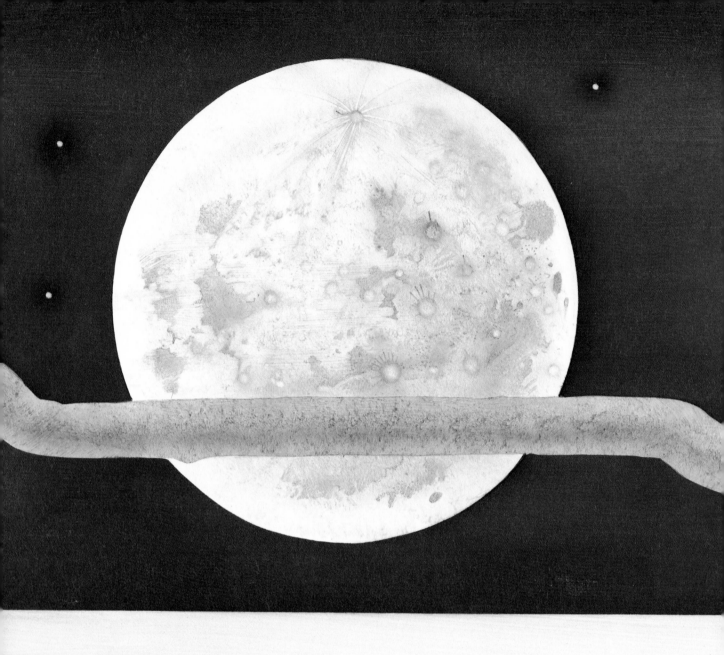

And when a moon floats on the sky

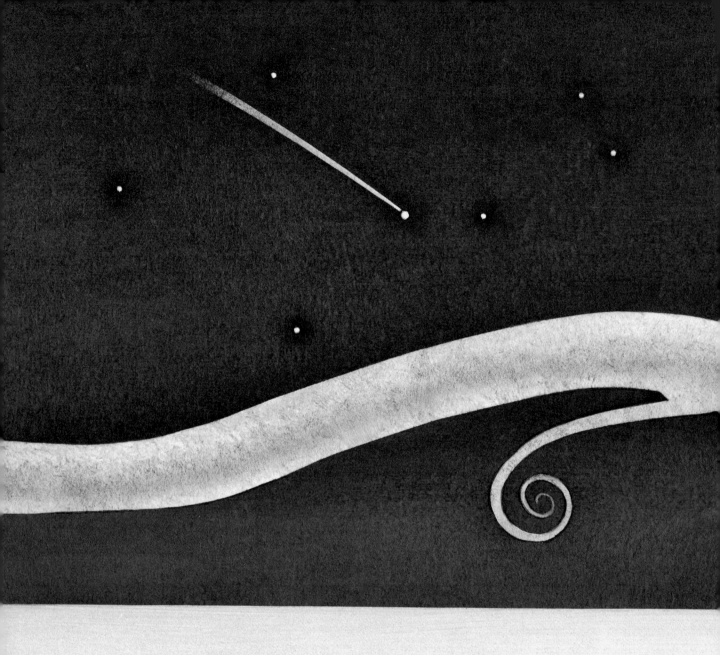

They hum a drowsy lullaby
Of sleepy children

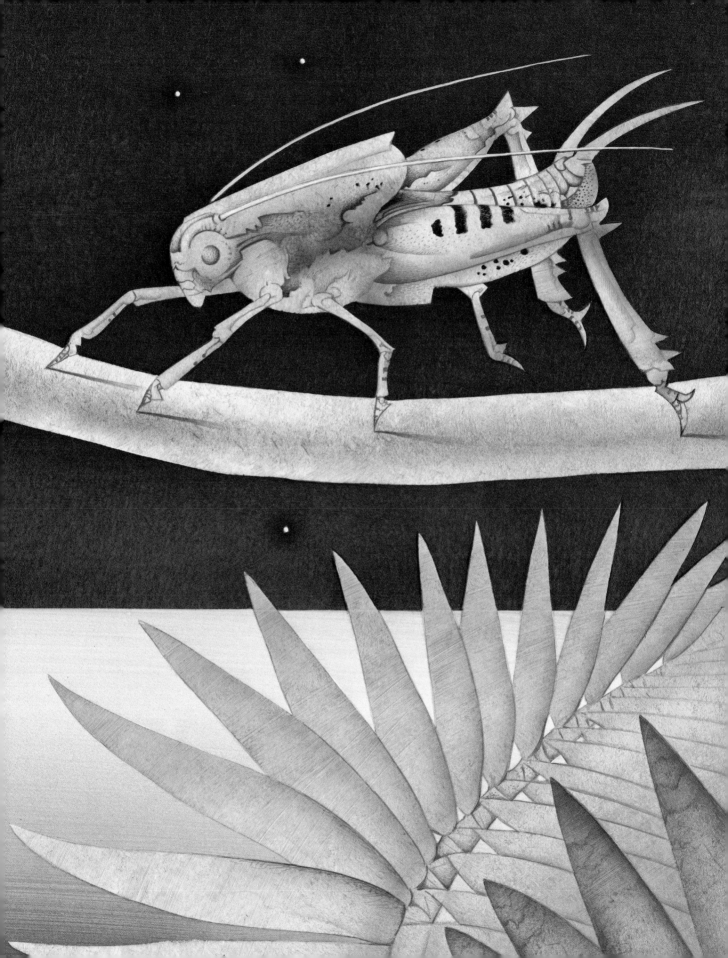

long ago . . .

Trees are the kindest things I know.

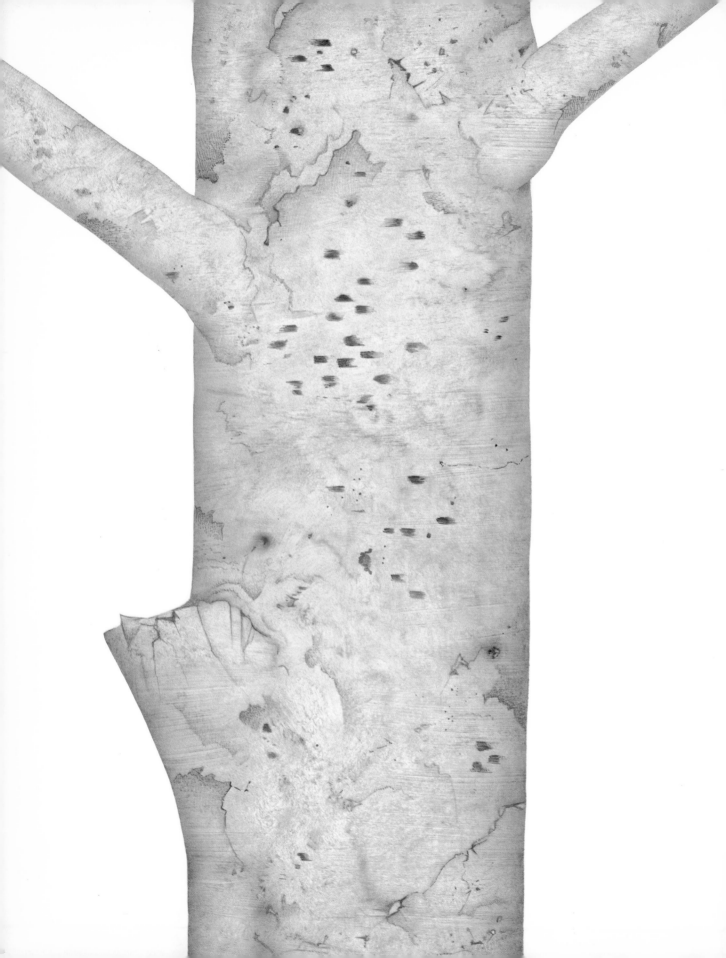

Bill Martin Jr, Ph.D., has devoted his life to the
education of young children. *Bill Martin Books* reflect
his philosophy: that children's imaginations are
opened up through the play of language, the imagery
of illustration, and the permanent joy of reading books.

First edition
Published by Henry Holt and Company, Inc.,
115 West 18th Street, New York, New York 10011.
Published simultaneously in Canada by Fitzhenry & Whiteside Ltd.,
195 Allstate Parkway, Markham, Ontario L3R 4T8.

Library of Congress Cataloging-in-Publication Data
Behn, Harry.
Trees : a poem / by Harry Behn ; illustrated by James Endicott.
"A Bill Martin book"
Summary: A poem celebrating the importance of trees.
ISBN 0-8050-1926-X
1. Trees—Juvenile poetry.   2. Children's poetry, American.
[1. Trees—Poetry.   2. American poetry.]
I. Endicott, James R., ill.   II. Title.
PS3503.E365T74   1992
811'.52—dc20   91-25179

Henry Holt books are available at special discounts
for bulk purchases for sales promotions, premiums,
fund-raising, or educational use. Special editions
or book excerpts can also be created to specification.

Printed in the United States of America
on 100% recycled, acid-free paper. ∞

10 9 8 7 6 5 4 3 2 1